HANDEL

HANDEL
BEFORE ENGLAND

by A. Craig Bell

Second impression 1976

DARLEY
THE GRIAN-AIG PRESS
1975

The Grian-aig Press
Darley, Harrogate
Yorkshire, England

Printed in Great Britain by
The Scolar Press Limited, Ilkley, Yorkshire

CONTENTS

HALLE
(1685 – 1703)

Like Mozart and Schubert, Handel began composing at a very early age, and if the compositions extant from the period of his apprenticeship to Zachau are as he wrote them, then he must be classed with those composers and Mendelssohn as being among the most amazing prodigies of music. A study of these very early works reveals that from the first Handel was the master of an innate sense of style. Not even Mozart had a surer feeling for outline or a purer melodic gift. The six trio-sonatas for two oboes and bassoon, supposedly written before he was in his teens, can charm us by their sheer stylistic excellence quite apart from the precocious contrapuntal skill displayed:

This gift of melody and sense of style was something which neither Zachau nor anyone else could teach him, for they are not teachable.

What the young Handel did get from him was a composer's proficiency on the organ and clavier and a comprehensive grounding in the science of composition – harmony, counterpoint, orchestration, choral writing. In addition, and just as important, through the Halle cantor's excellent library he made himself familiar not only with the styles of predecessors such as Carissimi, Frescobaldi and Froberger, but with contemporaries like Kerll, Krieger, Muffat and Pachelbel. So that when he left Halle and Zachau for Hamburg he was not only the most gifted musician of his time for his age, but the most knowledgeable in all the facets of his art. He remained grateful all his life to his only teacher; and when Zachau's widow fell on hard times he sent her 'frequent remittances' (in his first biographer's phrase).

His studies with Zachau lasted for eight years (1695 – 1703). In 1702 he was appointed probationary organist of Halle cathedral. But just when a secure way of life was opened to him, to the consternation of his family and friends he resigned the post and, throwing security to the winds, went off to face an uncertain future in Hamburg.

Biographers have found this step puzzling because it had no obvious purpose ('aimless' is Newman Flower's word for it). But because a motive is hidden it does not mean that it is any the less there; and while we can only read between the lines, (as we have to do so often with Handel, who gave nothing away about his aims and opinions) it seems clear that the young composer, with that quiet but unshakeable determination which perhaps was his most salient characteristic, had decided that he was not interested in becoming a typical German cantor. Unlike Buxtehude, Bach and César Franck, he knew that the organ loft and choir stalls were not his spiritual home, and the writing of endless church cantatas, as Zachau had insisted on his doing, no longer appealed to him. His nature was a restless one and demanded that, mentally and physically, he must stretch his legs periodically and seek pastures new. He felt constantly the itch to make himself familiar with other styles of music and other composers and musicians. This fact is borne out by the most cursory glance over his life, with its continual unrest and wanderings over the European continent. (The similar example of Mozart, with whom he has so much in common, springs at once to mind). Along with this innate restlessness went another equally salient characteristic: a fearless determination to be independent. Not even Beethoven had this trait and this strength of will and purpose more pronouncedly. Handel held only two official appointments all his life: the one at Halle already mentioned; and that of kapellmeister at the Hanoverian court – both of which were briefly and tenously held and thrown to the winds the moment he felt irked and constricted by them. Even at Cannons he was never 'employed' in the official sense. He was simply the 'composer in residence'. The official composer was the very minor Pepusch.

But why did he choose Hamburg, some two hundred miles away, it may be asked? The answer lay – for him – in the magical word: OPERA. Hamburg at that time was the operatic centre of Germany, and Handel's true vocation was beginning to call him with an ever-more insistent voice. So he threw up his job and its safe prospects and wandered off alone to Hamburg, like any of the heroes of fairy tale, to seek his fortune.

HAMBURG
(1703 – 1706)

Fortune, or luck, can be argued over endlessly. For one school of thought it is pre-ordained; for another it is pure chance; a third may subscribe to the theory that, given enough talent and character, a man can make his luck and ride it. Handel's career tempts one to put some faith in a mixture of the first and last belief; since wherever he went, and however 'aimless' and haphazard each move seemed to be, he invariably succeeded in achieving what he set out to achieve.

So in Hamburg. Here he met and associated with all the chief figures of the contemporary musical world gathered there: Reinken, Lubeck, Brade, Theile, Kusser, Reinhard Keiser, then the reigning operatic composer, and Mattheson. The last named has come to be closely associated with Handel. It was almost certainly he who got Handel the jobs of second violin in the opera orchestra and of harpsichord tutor to the son of the English consul, John Wyche; and of course he is peculiarly notorious for the famous quarrel ending in a duel in which Handel might well have lost his life but for the large metal button on his coat which shattered Mattheson's foil – symbol of the good fortune which hovered over Handel.

Handel did not waste his time. In the course of his three-year stay he wrote three operas – *Almira*, *Nero* and *Florinda und Daphne* – some chamber music, probably the three harpsichord suites in C, G and c minor (unpublished until 1930), his only sonata for viola da gamba, and (though again no certain date is ascribable) the three concertos for oboe, strings and continuo, together with the three 'Halle' sonatas for flute and bass.[1]

Of the operas, only *Almira* has come down to us, as the scores of the others are lost. It is not to be supposed that the first operatic venture of a composer of nineteen, however talented, would produce a masterpiece. Moreover, the libretto, 'a strange bi-lingual con-

---

[1]'During his continuance at Hamburg, he made a considerable number of sonatas. But what became of these pieces he never could learn, having been so imprudent as to let them go out of his hands'. (Mainwaring). See my *Chronological Thematic Catalogue* nos. 4, 5, 6, 7, 8, 11 for details of the above-mentioned works.

coction based on episodes in the life of Almira, Queen of Castille'[1] was against it from the start, and the score, by tradition and for current taste, had to include ballets and dance music rather after the style of Purcell's masques. Nevertheless, despite these weaknesses, while far from coming up to the London operas, *Almira* is well worth preserving both as a historical musical document and in its own right. The dance movements, consisting of *courantes, minuets, bourrées* and *sarabandes*, are thoroughly Handelian in their harmonic deftness and melodic grace. (All his life Handel loved writing dance music, seen at its most prolific in the later operas *Alcina* and *Ariodante*). With the final *sarabande* Handel knew he had written a winner, and he used it in two later works: the oratorio, *Il Trionfo del Tempo e del Disinganno* (1708), where he made it an aria to the words 'Lascia la spina', and the most famous of all, as the air 'Lascia ch'io pianga' in *Rinaldo* (1711).

Ex. 2

Additionally, the overture is full of Handelian finger-prints – the slow broad cantilena of the opening, followed by the jaunty *allegro* in his famous French overture style. But the highlights of the opera are the two soprano arias, one Italian, one German: 'Geloso tormento', sung by Almira, and 'Der Himmel Wird strafen' by Edilia. These could have been written at any time in Handel's career, and compare with the greatest arias of his London operas, anticipating as they do all that was to come in their respective energy and brilliance, harmonic originality and emotional depth. It will be observed that, typical in this, both arias are written for women (by far the greater part of his finest arias are for female characters) and inspired by strong emotions – in the one by fury and a desire for revenge; in the other by jealousy.

These two examples of baroque *aria* are well worth examining more closely if only to see the sort of music this nineteen-year old composer was turning out. The two arias are in complete contrast, as indeed they must be from the different emotions expressed. 'Geloso tormento' is the more complex and harmonically richer, as in fact an aria portraying jealousy with its clashing contrary emotions demands. The first thing to observe is the use of the oboe as the *obbligato* instrument. This was Handel's 'favourite instrument' in his early days, and is used here with all the poignant emotional over-

---

[1]James S. Hall, in *Handel* – the 'Great Master' series. (Boosey and Hawkes)

tones with which Bach was later to endow it. The second point is
that after the deeply expressive orchestral *ritornello* the voice enters
unaccompanied:

Ex. 3

Handel was to use this gambit time and time again:[1] it is one of
his finger-prints, and the reason for his doing it is simple and two-
fold, (1) as contrast with the orchestral sound, (2) more fundamentally and importantly, Handel understood as few other composers
the sheer emotive power of the voice. It was because of this understanding that he rarely felt the need – in contrast here to Bach,
essentially an instrumental composer – to weave counter-melodies
and complex figurations around his vocal line. I stress this because
so many academic text books, usually dating from round about the
1920's, make stale supererogatory remarks to the effect that Handel
is a 'simpler' composer than Bach and, because he did not write
intricate accompaniments to his airs and choruses, must be adjudged
as more 'slap-dash' and less 'thorough'.[2] Such nugatory comments
ignore the fact that Handelian simplicity calls for just as much
genius as Bachian complexity – a truth which Beethoven's well-
known observation on his favourite composer emphasised once and
for all. To Handel, before everything a singer's composer, with an

---

[1] Other noteable examples are: 'Sommi dei' (*Radamisto*), 'Care selve' (Atalanta),
'Come un rosa' (*Apollo e Dafne*), 'Total eclipse' (*Samson*). The unaccompanied
interjections in 'He was despised' in *Messiah* are extensions of the practice.
[2] The article in *The Oxford Companion* on Handel makes this pointless comparison.

unrivalled gift of melody, the voice was the core and centre of his inspiration, the keystone of his art. No other composer has come near to achieving such deceptively simple yet expressive music as 'O Sleep, why dost thou leave me?' (*Semele*), 'Care selve' (*Atalanta*), 'Verdi prati' (*Alcina*) or 'Total eclipse' (*Samson*). Bachian figuration in such instances, however splendid, would be totally out of place. The voice must glow in all the pristine beauty of *bel canto*, unhampered by instrumental competition. In all these and countless other instances, Handel's 'simplicity' is deliberate and not because he was 'indifferent', 'in a hurry', 'aiming at being easily understood' and other text book inanities. The most cursory study of the London opera scores will show that time and time again he could write accompaniment as complex as any of Bach's when he felt the music needed it.

To return to our aria. After the unaccompanied vocal entry on a rising octave, the oboe takes up its original 'lead', but now with the voice creating its own melody in counterpoint against it. The rising seventh here, followed by the rising octave four bars later, releasing almost surcharged emotion, is another Handelian finger-print, illustrating his almost instinctive knowledge from the very beginning of the expressive potential of the voice.

Ex. 4

We meet this finger-print frequently in later works, one of the finest examples occurring in the *Salve Regina* of 1707. (See page 34). The first section closes with the opening orchestral *ritornello*. The *da capo*, only two bars shorter and in the relative major, extends and heightens the emotion. In it, too, are to be found carefully indicated and unusual variations in dynamics, (*ps.* being followed by sudden *fs.* and vice versa), dramatic tension and harmonic surprises. I quote the last eight bars to show this, and the extraordinary 'close':

Ex. 5

di ge-lo-si-a tra le mor - - ti e la peg - gior, tra le morti e la peg-

-gior ch'il mo-rir di ge-lo-si-a tra le morti, tra le morti e la peg-gior.

The aria is one of the shortest to be found in any of the operas, being only thirty-six bars in all; but it is one of the most intense and expressive.

The opening *ritornello* of the German aria, with its strident unisons (another finger-print) followed by the onward-driving bass line foretells its style and character:

Ex. 6 (Allegro spiritoso)

The handling of the orchestra, in which he was far ahead of contemporaries such as Bononcini and A. Scarlatti (as with Mozart later, he was criticised for the 'noisiness' of his accompaniments) is one of the reasons why his cantatas sound so much more advanced than theirs.

Again following the *ritornello* the voice enters unaccompanied (from F² to B♭²!):

After this the musical sentence is repeated but lengthened by a phrase, and proceeds by means of a testing piece of *coloratura*:

The climax of the first section comes just before the end with a superb octave leap:

and the aria ends:

The *da capo* section, far from being shorter as so many are, is just as long and dramatic, and technically even more difficult. Two climactic C's,[2] led up to by skilful preparation, show that even at this early stage Handel knew all about the singer's art.

Ex. 11

ver‑stür‑en,   ver‑kehr‑en,   ver‑seh‑ren,   ver‑heer‑en,

Ex. 12

ver‑stür‑en,   ver‑keh‑ren   ver‑seh‑ren,   ver‑heer‑en,

The section is brought to a close in a succession of rising trills ranging over a ninth to end in d minor, making the B*b* *reprise* a typical example of Handel's sense of harmonic 'colour'.

Ex. 13

- zicht,——————————————————————— dess Ruh' und Vergnügung sich dein‑er ent‑zicht.

Such a *bravura* aria must have brought the house down, one feels; and also prompts the reflection that the Hamburg opera must have been blessed with outstanding singers.

A final point to be made after a study of the opera is that it proclaims not only a born composer for the voice but for the orchestra too. No doubt the inside practical knowledge of orchestral technique acquired from his second violin desk helped; but a dozen composers could sit there and fail to achieve that subtle fusion between stage and pit which is so vital before an opera can become a work of unified art. Like Mozart, Handel had this birthright from the start, whereas it took Gluck, Verdi and Wagner years before they mastered it. *Almira* represents Handel's first really important step towards his true goal, and was his first resounding success – so much so, it is said, as to have made Keiser, the accepted king of Hamburg opera, desperately jealous.

His next operas, *Nero* and *Florinda und Daphne*, did not meet with anything like the acclaim of *Almira;* but whether this was on account of the music or of extraneous circumstances we do not know, since the scores are unfortunately lost.

Of the other compositions dating from this period (see page 4) the masterpiece is the C major suite for harpsichord.[1] The magnificent *Prelude* (a most originally conceived combination of prelude and

---

[1]Recorded by Mary Verney ('Handel and his Contemporaries' – Jupiter).

fugue), along with the equally fine *Allemande* of the c minor suite,[1]
is very Bachian – always a sign that it must have come from the
young Handel before he shed the German-cantor influence.

Ex. 14

This, after continuing its fluent course for 31 bars, without a
break unexpectedly foliates into a 4-part fugue.

Ex. 15

But its crowning glory is the chaconne.

Ex. 16

This is arguably Handel's keyboard masterpiece, and takes its
place with the greatest baroque keyboard works. Certainly it stands
far and above the better known G major chaconne of the second
volume of the Suites (no. 10) and belongs to that series of historically
important examples of variation form stretching from Bull (*Walsing-
ham*), Bach (*Goldberg*) and Haydn (*Andante varié in f minor*) to the
monumental creations of Beethoven and Brahms. Here is a Handel
determined to give the harpsichordist 'something to think about', to
quote Beethoven's half humorous comment on his 'Hammerclavier'
sonata. Some of the variations display a marvellous variety of
rhythm, and call for a professional finger technique:

---

[1]Almost identical with the *Allemande* of the Schott 1928 publication – *G. F. Handel:
Pieces for Harpsichord*. (See vol. 2, page 27).

Ex. 17

And number 21 recalls the Spanish rhythms of D. Scarlatti:

Ex. 18

But the pinnacle of the variations is to be found in numbers 36 – 40. The sliding chromatic progressions give them astonishingly ambivalent tonality, a subtle hovering between major and minor that is audaciously original for its period and anticipatory of the 'romanticism' of Schubert and others. It was a stroke of sheer genius by which, when he came to enlarge the work to forty-nine variations[1] (a proof he must have thought highly of it), Handel inserted a minor version of the theme:

Ex. 19

and followed it by a variation in which the upward-sliding passing notes in the l.h. anticipate those of the already composed vn. 38 which are in the r.h.

---

[1]There are two versions of this chaconne: one with twenty-seven variations, the other with forty-nine. When Handel revised the work is not known, as no autograph of it exists. The forty-nine variation version was first published by Schott in 1928; the twenty-seven variation version by Bärenreiter in 1930. My references are taken from the former.

Quite apart from its intrinsic inspiration and importance, the chaconne spiritually and technically anticipates and is hauntingly suggestive of Beethoven's 32 c minor variations. Not only are the two eight-bar themes themselves similar, but certain variations are notationally alike.

Where Beethoven, his theme being minor, goes for contrast into the major, Handel's, being in the major, goes minor. Of course, Beethoven cannot have known this chaconne, which astonishingly remained unpublished until this century (although he may have been familiar with the G major one of the suites); but this fact only emphasises the indigenous affinity between the two composers, whose fundamental technical expression is based firmly on diatonic scale and chord principle, structure, and use of elemental blocks of tonal sound: hence one of the reasons for Beethoven's preference for Handel above all composers. Not only so, but here Beethoven (like Mendelssohn in his masterpiece *Variations Sérieuses*) harks back to the Handelian principle of variation, viz. melodic development over a reiterated harmonic foundation. This work alone shows that Beethoven's affinity with Handel was closer than it was with Bach.

In the autumn of 1706 Handel left Hamburg for Italy as abruptly as he had left Halle for Hamburg. This again has puzzled some biographers, though the reasons are similar. Clearly he felt he had learned all that Keiser and the hybrid Hamburg opera could teach him, and that no further progress or benefit was possible there. Then with that clarity of vision and ability to size up a situation which was another of his characteristics, in all probability he foresaw in the growing opposition of the Pietists (the German equivalent of our Puritans) the death knell of Hamburg opera. (This did in fact come about towards the end of the 1730's when Handel was in England, partly owing to religious intolerance and opposition, and partly through its own meretricious standards).

In any case Italy called him with a siren voice – the voice of *bel canto* and that of Steffani whom he had met and whose typical Italian *cantilena* he had come to admire. To musicians then, as to poets and artists later, Italy was the radiant centre of the world. To the Eldorado of European music, therefore, in Mainwaring's delightful 18th century English, 'he resolved to go on his own bottom as soon as he could make a purse for that occasion'.

ITALY
(1706 – 1710)

No doubt he had introductions; but as always Handel met new acquaintances on equal terms and made his way by sheer hard work, determination and genius. After studying the principal pre-contemporary and contemporary Italian composers very thoroughly he began composing in earnest. In fact he must, to use his own words, have 'worked like the devil', for his output over the three and a half years of his stay was phenomenal, even by his own standards. It comprises: the *Dixit Dominus*, *Nisi Dominus*, D major *Laudate pueri*, *Salve Regina*, *Donna che in Ciel*, eight large-scale antiphons, twenty-two cantatas for various voices and instruments, seventy-four cantatas for solo voice and continuo, seven *Airs Francois*, two *Italian Duetti* and *Terzetti*, two oratorios, two operas and a serenata. The mere list is impressive. When one adds to it the fact that some of the works are among the highlights of his compositions, it becomes something to wonder at. This Italian period has come to be regarded by many historians as 'experimental', 'assimilative', 'formative', and so on. It began that way, of course, but it soon became much more. Inspired by the Italian language and by Italian singers and melody, surrounded by admiring musicians and composers such as Corelli, the Scarlattis and others, stimulated by them and literary Cardinal friends like Colonna, Ottoboni and Pamfili, who wrote libretti for him, above all by his chief patron, Prince Ruspoli,[1] his genius burgeoned like a plant nurtured in ideal conditions. The three years spent in Italy formulated his style, his melodic and harmonic techniques. His Italian experience had an incalculable effect on his genius, and haunted him to the end of his days. The

---

[1]Handel's position in the Ruspoli household was similar to his later appointment to the Duke of Chandos at Cannons. He was not the official kapellmeister (Antonio Caldar was that), but he was expected to contribute to the many various occasions, religious and secular, which arose. Or in Mainwaring's words: 'Handel was desired to furnish his quota' – which for quite a period of time included one cantata every Sunday for his patron's *conversaziones*. For this and other interesting details see the article. 'The Ruspoli Documents' by Ursula Kirkendale in the 'Journal of the American Musicological Society' for 1964.

Italianate Handel took over from the German-cantor Handel and, after *Dixit Dominus,* obliterated him. Even the 'English' Handel never excluded the Italian (*Acis and Galatea* is a perfect fusion). The earlier inspiration kept creeping in. Thus even the late *Susanna* contains a quotation from the cantata *Tu fedel? tu costante?* And his ultimate opus, *The Triumph of Time and Truth,* was fundamentally a reworked version of his 1708 *Il Trionfo del Tempo.*

For the sake of convenience the Italian works can be classified under five headings: secular cantata, church music, oratorio, opera, vocal chamber music: and I propose to discuss them in that order.

The exact order of the hundred-odd cantatas is impossible to define. The writing of them must have been spread over the greater part of Handel's stay in Italy. The *raison d'être* of these works and of the cantata as a musical form is curious and interesting.

The Italian cantata was an elusive compound of opera, oratorio and serenata. A 'mini' off-spring of these larger-scale forms, like them it developed from a comparatively simple succession of recitatives with accompaniment of a keyboard instrument and bass into a hybrid opera-serenata-oratorio with orchestral accompaniment containing ever-increasing numbers of arias and less and less recitative. Unlike opera the cantata was unacted, and so became a form of salon entertainment. By the time Handel burst on to the Italian scene the cantata had been raised to a recognised art form moulded by the successive hands of Carissimi, Stradella, Pergolesi, Bononcini and above all, Alessandro Scarlatti – the last-named writing almost as many cantatas as his son Domenico wrote sonatas. Indeed the form had become so ubiquitous and popular that one may fairly claim that it was to the 18th century what the string quartet and other forms of chamber music were to the 19th century. Handel was encouraged – indeed almost coerced – to add to the already extensive repertoire by the fact that not long before his advent the Pope banned all opera, partly because he considered it meretricious, and partly as a show of power and displeasure in that despite his edict, opera had been performed during Lent and other self-sacrificial periods. This must have been a bitter blow to Handel, who had regarded Italy as the promised land of opera. However, no doubt seeing in these chamber cantatas the germs of operatic possibility and an outlet for his dramatic instinct, and urged on by wealthy artistic patrons like Prince Ruspoli and Cardinal Ottoboni who were much too opera-addicted to renounce their chief form of pleasure, Handel set about providing them with his own versions of the popular form. Posterity is fortunate that he did so: they contain some of his most characteristic and original music.

Basing them on the examples by A. Scarlatti, he surpassed his model as he was to surpass (like Mozart) every model. Scarlatti's cantatas, though beautiful and attractive, tend to lack diversity and character.[1] Handel's may be less perfect formally, but they are stamped over-all with a more powerful personality, are more adventurous melodically and harmonically, and, above all, they are more dramatic.

These cantatas can be divided into two groups: those for solo voice and continuo, and those for various voices and instruments. The former consist only of a bass (sometimes figured, sometimes not) and the vocal line. But what basses they are! These powerful generic 'roots' allow us a fascinating glimpse into the composer's workshop; almost to see in a flash of revelation the creative process in actual fermentation.

Ex. 23 (Cantata No. 11 - 'Del bell' idolo mio')
Andante

Ex. 24 (Cantata No. 43 -'Non sospirar, non piangero')
Adagio

Ex. 25 (Cantata No. 44 - 'Occhi miei che faceste?')
Adagio

Built on basses of such generic and emotive power, the super-structure could not fail to produce something above the ordinary run-of-the-mill cantata; and in fact those from which the above examples are taken are among the finest of his compositions of any period. For not only are the basses superb, but the vocal line evoked by them is frequently just as astonishing in its originality, concentration and expressiveness. The two following examples illustrate this:

---

[1]Though in fairness to Scarlatti it should be stated that a mere fraction of his vast output is available, and judgment is necessarily based on the little that is known.

Ex. 26 (Cantata No. 11 'Del bell' idolo mio')

(Note the melismatic 'sigh' of the vocal entry inspired by the 'un sospir') *No. 68 – 'Un sospir a chi si muore'*:

Ex. 27

Harmonically perhaps the most original of all is the *adagio* of number forty-five ('*O lucenti, o sereni occhi*'). The brief (eight-bar) but intense D.C. section is worth quoting in full:

Ex. 28

One wonders how Handel's contemporaries and audiences reacted to what must have seemed such avant-garde music. Noticeable is the fact that the majority of the movements are slow in tempo (*largo* or *adagio*) and in minor key (g minor is the most favoured). A detailed study of these cantatas (and they deserve no less) cannot fail to bring home to any musician (1) that he is in the presence of one of the greatest masters of polyphony that ever lived (2) the truth of Rameau's contention that 'melody is born of harmony'. For here is Handel at his most daring and experimental, revelling in grinding harmonic clashes, startling melodic progressions and modulations, expressive melismata, chromaticism and unexpected intervals (seconds and augmented fourths abound). These cantatas display the young composer rejoicing in new-found strength, manipulating his material like wind and weather on a tree shaping it to their will. If those musicians and musicologists who reserve their more fulsome superlatives for Bach and ignore Handel had taken the trouble to examine these works (and others) they would have found in them all they rave over as unique in the Leipzig cantor. The difference being that where Bach by and large needed religion for his stimulus, Handel the dramatic composer and humanist found his in the passions of human beings – even in vague historical characters and imaginary shepherds and shepherdesses. While Bach's assertion that music should be composed to the glory of God would doubtless have obtained his support, Handel like Mozart, Schubert and Brahms after him, even more firmly believed that music should first and formost give pleasure to human beings.

Great as the above-noted cantatas are, the apotheosis of them is to be found in *Lucrezia* ('O Numi eterni!'). Some idea of the range of its emotional gamut can be gauged from the scale of the work which, in the edition of Michael Tippett and Walter Bergmann[1] runs to seventeen pages, and in the course of which there are to be found no less than ten changes of mood and tempo. The plan is: *Recitative – aria (adagio) – recitative – aria (allegro) – recitative – furioso – aria (adagio) – recitative – arioso – furioso*. In the first *recitative* Lucretia appeals to the 'eternal Gods' to avenge the outrage perpetrated against her by Tarquin. In the f minor *adagio* she reflects pathetically on her shame, now blazoned abroad, and implores the Gods to give her their aid and consolation. The second *recitative*, still more passionate, declares her to be prepared to invoke the Gods of Hell if those of Heaven remain deaf to her prayers. She then bursts into a furious curse against her ravisher, calling down ruin and destruction on his head. The third *recitative* reveals her

---

[1]Published by Schott, and recorded by Janet Baker (Philips).

wavering doubts: if heaven refuses her aid, is it likely that hell will
grant it? And if so, would not remorse come to punish her and make
her, the victim, suffer? She now takes the dagger in her hand, and
the anticipation of her own death as the sole way out of her torment
is told in the extraordinarily chromatic g minor *larghetto* with its
quasi-fugal dialogue between voice and bass:

Ex. 29

The *arioso* which precedes the final impassioned *furioso* is in some
ways the most daringly original section of the work. Beginning
firmly in the key of E*b* major immediately after the f minor full
close of the preceding *recitative*, it gropes desperately for six bars
along with Lucrezia's almost incoherent mental state (a magnificent
example, this, of dramatic psychology), throwing baroque tonality
to the winds before finding the home key again – which it leaves
immediately to work its tortuous way via *recitative* to a close in the
tonic key of the piece – f minor.

Ex. 30

fer - ro   i   du - riuf - fi - - - - - - zü;

The foregoing brief description gives only the barest inkling of the overwhelming intensity of this tremendous *scena*. From the opening bars of the first *recitative* to the hammer blows of the last chords, the music scales the highest peaks of inspiration. Only occasionally in the London operas and oratorios was Handel to write music of the tragic force of this monodrama which, in addition to its own intrinsic worth, is the direct heir of the great solo *scenas* of Purcell (*Mad Bess, The Blessed Virgin's Expostulation*) and the progenitor of the later ones of Haydn (*Scena di Berenice*), Beethoven (*Ah, perfido!*), Weber, Mendelssohn and others.

The chamber cantatas, although superficially more attractive in that the orchestral accompaniment and the employment (in some instances) of more than one voice help to make them easier on the ear, are more unequal from a strictly musical criterion. The instrumental colour enables the young composer to relax and to have the musical thought carried along rather too much *al fresco* on occasions. Thus (to cite a typical example) the Sinfonia of No. 1 (*Ah! crudel, nel pianto mio*), opening with a theme which he was to use (slightly varied) in no less than four later works, is allowed to amble a little too discursively.[1]

Ex. 31

The tonality of the arias, too, seems arbitrary, ranging through e minor, c minor, b minor and G major. Similar criticism applies to the two cantatas 'a tre', viz. nos. 19 (*O! come chiare e belle*) and 24 (*Clori, Tirzi, Fileno*) – the first consisting of nine arias and a final trio; the second, though incomplete, of eight arias, three duets and a final trio – miniature operas indeed! However, if this is on the debit side, on the credit side must be placed a far-reaching bid for

---

[1] This found its ultimate expression in the haunting yet elusive *Air in A major* for harpsichord, recently published by Bärenreiter and recorded by Luciano Sgrizzi (Errato).

originality and a positive eagerness for experiment. In this respect
these cantatas can be seen as a try-out, a sort of experimental
station for ideas and forms which were to find their apotheosis in
the later operas. Thus in no. 12 (*Delirio amoroso*) he introduces both
oboe and flute, a violoncello *obbligato*, bravura unaccompanied
passages for solo violin and a purely instrumental minuet. Perhaps
the most original of all – a little self-consciously so, one feels – is
no. 24, cited above. The music may not be Handel at his most
distinguished, but how the exuberant young composer is spreading
himself and revelling in it!

Ex. 32

Ex. 33 Presto (ma non prestissimo)

With 'Un sospiretto, un labbro pallido'[1] comes the first of his
lilting waltz rhythms

Ex. 34 Andante

and the next aria is the exhilarating 'Come la rondinella'[2] with its
arciluto *obbligato*.

---

[1]This, like the aria '*Hò un non sò che nel cor*' in *La Resurrezione*, was such a 'hit', that
Handel used it again in no. 67 of the solo cantatas *Udite il mio consiglio* (or perhaps
vice versa, precise composition dates being unknown), and as the aria 'Allor che
sorge' in *Rodrigo* (1709) and *Il Pastor Fido* (1712).
[2]Recorded by Bernadette Greevy and Raymond Leppard ('Handel Arias'–Argo).

Ex. 35

And in the final aria of *Tu fedel? tu costante?* we have the delightful hemiola:

Ex. 36

Of them all, however, no. 3 (*Arresta il passo*) wins hands down for sheer exuberance and a Haydnesque humour that comes near to clowning. (It is often forgotten that Handel had a keen, if rather sardonic, sense of humour). After fourteen bars of a typical stately French overture the music erupts into

which after pursuing its headlong course for thirty-seven bars is
dramatically and high-handedly arrested and silenced in mid-flight
by the entry of the voice:

Ex. 38

After an aria in B*b* a *recitative* takes the tonality into b minor, and
this is followed by the aria 'Fiamma belle' in seductive waltz rhythm
and G major!

Ex. 39

Again, Handel (perhaps his audiences too) liked this so much
that he repeated it with very slight alterations as 'Ogni venti' in
Agrippina. But it is with the aria 'Fu scherzo, fu gioco' that the fun
begins. The opening instrumental *ritornello* sounds like a baroque
version of *Lady Badinscott's Reel* – that jaunty Scottish air to which
Burns set the equally jaunty words 'My love she's but a lassie yet':

Ex. 40

But after five bars this rhythm gives way to an extended series of
triplets played by violins I and II in thirds against the eight-quaver
bass, and the *ritornello* ends with a compromise between the two.
The voice pursues this compromise:

Ex. 41

Fu scher-zo, fu   gio - co chi dis - se cheil fo - co del nu - me di   Gni - do

Thereafter the violins dog the voice like hounds on the scent, sometimes playing in thirds with it, or in unison, or almost mockingly echoing it. But the climax to the clowning comes in the final duet which is not only brilliant, but true *buffo*, and could claim to be a 'patter song' a hundred years before Rossini and nearly two hundred before Sullivan.[1] First Aminta has the 'patter' while Fillide gives her harmonic support:

Ex. 42

Aminta

Per ab-bat - ter il   ri-go-re d'un crudel   spie -ta - to co - re,   per ab-

Fillide

per ab - bat -ter il ri-go-re d'un crudel - -

-bat-ter il ri-go-re d'un crudel spietato core, per ab- bat-ter il ri-go-re d'un crudel spietato core d'un cru-

- - spie - ta - - - - - - -

Then follows a passage in which they 'patter' in unaccompanied thirds, after which the roles are reversed and Aminta sings the suspensions over Fillide's 'patter':

Ex. 43

-lor di fedeltà,   for -   - te   scu

-lor di fedeltà,   per abbatter il rigore d'un crudel spietato core, forte

[1]The jingle runs:

> Per abbatter il rigore
> d'un crudel spietato core
> forte scudo è la costanza
> e il valor di fedeltà.

The D.C. section pursues the *buffo* character with comic unisons between the voices and violins:

One can visualise the smile on Handel's face as he wrote it. The whole cantata is a splendid *tour de force* which should be made public property. It would bring the house down.

One of the most formally satisfying cantatas is no. 10 – *Crudel tiranno Amor;*[1] for not only is the music itself of high quality, but its construction is tauter. Its three movements (*allegro – larghetto – allegro*, bridged by *recitatives*) correspond to the principle of sonata form where most of the others approximate to the more heterogeneous suite. As if to further guarantee self-discipline, Handel has confined his instrumentation to strings. While each of the movements has its own perfection, the *larghetto* ('O dolce mia speranza') particularly haunts the memory:

---

[1] Recorded by Elly Ameling (Phillips).

It is, in fact, a *siciliana* – a form which Handel was to use so extensively (usually in a minor key) as to make it peculiarly his own. There is scarcely one of his London operas which does not contain at least one ravishing example. This one, with its subtle modulations and orchestral interjections, so simple and yet so eloquent, is a typical illustration.[1]

Armida abbandonata[2] is another outstanding cantata, with its *arpeggiando* first violins in the opening *recitativo*, its moving *adagio* ('Ah! crudele'), its accompanied *recitativo* (*furioso*) 'O voi, dell' incostante e procelloso mare', its turbulent 'Venti, fermate, sì' and expressive concluding *siciliana*. Bach thought highly enough of the work to copy and study it.

Nevertheless, the masterwork among these cantatas is *Apollo e Dafne*.[3] In it invention, control, melody and orchestration meet to fashion one of the most perfect works to come from Handel's Italian pen. The libretto is based on the Greek legend of Dafne who, pursued by the amorous Apollo, was changed by Diana into a laurel tree. In the opening *recitative* and *aria* Apollo boasts that Greece owes its liberation solely to him for slaying the monster which has been terrifying the land; and here Handel proclaims in advance the care he intends to lavish on his instrumentation, which consists of flute, two oboes, bassoon, strings and continuo. In the course of the aria's orchestral *ritornello*, where in his English oratorios he would almost certainly have left everything to the strings, he meticulously interchanges strings and woodwind:

Ex. 46

In the next *recitative* Apollo boasts still more, declaring scornfully that Cupid, who merely wounds lovers, is not to be compared with him. In the *aria* 'Spezza l'arco e getta l'armi' which, in its mock-martial style anticipates the famous 'Non più andrai' of Figaro, he arrogantly tells Cupid to break his bow and arrows since they have

---

[1]Handel evidently thought highly enough of it to transfer it bodily into the opera *Floridante* for Rossane's aria to the same words.

[2]Recorded by Janet Baker (E.M.I.).

[2]Recorded by Bruce Boyce/Margaret Ritchie (Oiseau – Lyre) and Fischer-Dieskau/Agnes Giebel (D.G.).

no chance of touching him. Glory and arms are everything, love a boy's matter. The scoring for oboes and bassoon is exquisite:

Ex. 47

But Apollo having had his say, it is Dafne's turn. And what a turn! If I were asked to name from the some thousand arias of Handel my prime favourite, while rejecting the bare possibility of making any such choice, this *siciliana*, 'Felicissima quest 'alma' would be in my select short-list. It is indeed one of the most magical and moving Handel ever wrote, not only by reason of its sheer melodic beauty, but also because of the imaginative and original orchestration, being scored for solo oboe and pizzicato strings (with the exception of the double-bass which sustains the bass-line *arco*). The total result is a sensuous beauty of sound of which Handel was to become so supreme a master. I should like to quote the whole of the aria, but must content myself with the introductory *ritornello* and the first bars of the soprano entry:

Ex. 48

Hearing such a song, it is no wonder Apollo is made to exclaim
'Che voce! che beltà!' and to go back on his words and confess the
melting power of music, the food of love. But in the d minor aria
'Ardi ardori' (with solo violin and oboe)[1] Dafne repulses him,
declaring she will remain constant to Diana and her vow of chastity.
In a spirited duet (*à la gigue*) the two express their emotions, after
which follows the second highlight of the cantata: a deeply expressive
recitative and *aria* from Apollo. The former, with compelling chord
sequences supporting the emotionally charged vocal line, displays
Handel's dramatic mastery. From the chord of f ♯ minor the aria
begins in the relative major (a perfect example of Handel's sense of
colour) with great sighs from the violins to the accompaniment of a
solo violoncello: but the voice on its entry is unaccompanied –
another masterstroke.

Ex. 49

---

[1]The opening orchestral *ritornello* anticipates the Trio 'The flocks shall leave the
mountains' in *Acis and Galatea*

The sentiment of the aria can be summed up by the well-known poem of Herrick: *Gather Ye Rosebuds While Ye May*. 'Like a lovely rose', sings Apollo in one of the most tender and haunting love songs ever written for a baritone, 'your beauty will soon perish, leaving you forlorn. Love while you may'. The *da capo*, as beautiful as the first and longer section, ends in c♯ minor, to make the A major *reprise* a thing of even greater beauty. Baritone arias of such lyrical tenderness are rare, and should be treasured accordingly.

But, evidently not as responsive to the power of music as Apollo, Dafne is not moved to any relenting, and in her subsequent aria – a lovely *siciliana* in g minor 'Come in ciel benigna stella' – she renews her vow to remain faithful to Diana. Here again Handel reveals quite startling originality. The orchestra plays in 12/8 but the time signature for the voice is 4/4, and this deliberate cross-rhythm, anticipating Mozart (K.456) and Brahms, is maintained for the greater part of the first section of the aria:

Ex. 50

Apollo renews his ardour in a short *adagio* accompanied by solo flute; but, adamant, Dafne declares she will die rather than yield. Apollo swears he will possess her, and Dafne flees from him. The chase is depicted in Apollo's triumphant 'Mie piante correte', preluded and accompanied by a *sinfonia* of scurrying strings, solo violin and bassoon:

Ex. 51

But just as Apollo is about to seize her, she is changed into a laurel, and the cantata concludes with a sarabande-like aria sung by the now-repentant god, who declares he will wear the leaves round his brow and that the tree shall become a symbol of honour and renown for evermore. The work is a masterpiece.

To sum up. These Italian cantatas can be seen in a double light: as studies for the operas to come; and as highly original works in their own right. As regards the former aspect, Handel must have realised their dramatic potential, for he carefully brought his scores to England with him when he finally decided to live in this country, and cannily used them as a store house into which to dip – either re-using some of the arias lock, stock and barrel, or re-shaping them, according to his fancy. From the second aspect, varying in quality though they do, they are proofs of his adaptability and originality. Within the same stereotyped framework they abound in endless suprises, daring experiment, inexhaustible melodic fecundity, uninhibited harmonic boldness, a born dramatic sense and sensitivity to orchestral colour. They should be republished from the Handel-Gesellschaft and made more widely known.[1] There is some magnificent music for singers here.

---

[1]The only ones published are: – *Nel dolce dell' oblio* and *Lucrezia* (Schott), *Spanish Cantata* (Broekman en van Poppel), and *La Solitudine, Tra le fiamme, Tu fedel? tu costante? Dalla guerra amorosa* (all by Bärenreiter).

To come now to the church music. This, in its turn, can be divided conveniently into two groups: the antiphons, and the larger-scale works, *Dixit Dominus, Nisi Dominus* and the *Laudate pueri.*

The former comprise: *Donna che in ciel, Salve Regina, Coelestis dum spirat, O qualis de coelo, Haec est Virginem,*[1] *Te decus Virginem,*[2] *Saeviat Tellus inter vigores,* and *Ah! che troppo ineguali,* composed at the special request of Handel's friend and patron, Cardinal Colonna and first performed in the church of Santa Maria as part of the 1708 celebrations for the deliverance of Rome from the earthquakes which devastated the area in 1702 – 1703.[3] That such essentially Catholic compositions should be written by one who had been, and in essence remained, a Lutheran, is remarkable to say the least. The question immediately arises – are they to be attributed merely to a wish to honour his Italian friends and to prove to them that a foreigner and Protestant could beat them at their own game? Or are they the result of a sudden, if temporary, conversion? We shall never know the answer, for Handel, the most impersonal and unself-conscious of geniuses, left no letters or any confession which might give us a clue to his feelings or opinions on any religious or personal matters whatever. But even if we did not know that he was urged to become a convert,[4] it would be difficult to believe that friends and patrons such as Corelli, the Scarlattis, Pasquini, Prince Gastone and the three Cardinals did not do their utmost, in the friendliest way possible, to bring so illustrious a 'heretic' into the fold of what they believed to be 'the true church'.[5] Surrounded by a Catholic hierarchy, steeped in its music, allowed to perform on the organ in the church of Saint John Lateran (an unheard of privilege in those times for a Protestant), commissioned by Princes and Cardinals to provide their churches, opera houses and salons with musical entertainment, and moreover being at an age most open to influence from the climate of opinion in which he found himself, it would not be surprising if he had been influenced to some degree. This is, of course, pure supposition, but the works composed at this time are hard fact, and lend colour to the possibility. Never again was he to compose in so Italianly Catholic a vein. Not only so, but almost all these works display an intensity of feeling expressed through music of such extraordinary poignancy as to be almost lacerating.

---

[1]Music lost.
[2]Unpublished.
[3]See my *Chronological Thematic Catalogue,* nos. 16 – 21.
[4]Through his first biographer – Mainwaring.
[5]Handel's own remark made in his later years, that what he most liked about England and the English was the fact that no one was pressed to hold any particular belief, may also be an oblique reference to his experience in Italy.

So that again one asks: can such effects be achieved objectively by means of technique alone and a desire to emulate and surpass, or can it come only from spiritual conviction? As regards the former supposition, there is this factor to take into account: the Italy of this era was an artist's and composer's Eldorado, with a venerable and venerated tradition going back through Alessandro Scarlatti, Corelli, Carissimi, Stradella and others to Monteverdi and Palestrina. Italian patrons and audiences were conditioned into expecting and accepting only the best. The young Handel understood this very well, and because he did so and was at the beginning of his career, he was driven by expectation, competition and almost by necessity to give the best that was in him. To stake his claim by anything less would have been a sacrilege. To be considered a second-best was unbearable to him all through his career. To the end he had to be both in his own esteem and in that of others *primus inter pares*. Neither in Italy nor in England did he tolerate a rival near his throne.

Of the antiphons in honour of the Virgin, *Donna che in ciel*[1] is the most ambitious, though by no means the finest, consisting of three arias and recitatives and a final chorus. The highlights are the second aria, 'Tu sei la bella serena stella', in which the profound simplicity of the later opera arias is anticipated but not quite attained, and the chorus which, begun by the soloist, is taken over by the choir in ever-growing tension. And a point of interest for the Handel student may be found in the fact that its generic *motif* is to be found again in the c minor 'Aria' for harpsichord in the so-called *Aylesford Pieces* – reminding us that from the very first Handel's themes were equally instrumental and vocal:

Ex. 52

(Allegro)

Ma - ri - a,   sa - lu - te   espe - - - me,

The two masterworks of the collection are the two smallest in scale: the *Salve Regina* and the *Ah! che troppo ineguali*.[2] The former, with its echoes of Carissimi and Monteverdi, its astonishing harmonic ventures, its fully written organ part and its rarified atmosphere, may be said to stand as the apotheosis of these Romish compositions. The *adagio* and *adagissimo* movements are especially striking. In the course of the former we find one of Handel's most powerful examples of the

---

[1]Published by Arno Volk Verlag, Köln.
[2]Recorded by Elly Ameling (BASF/Harmonia Mundi Records).

characteristic emotionally charged 'soaring' effect of the rising
interval which he had captured in his very first operatic essay (see
page 7); only here it is the ultimate of it – a minor ninth. This
occurs no less than four times in the span of the movement's sixty-
eight bars, twice in the orchestral part, and twice repeated by the
voice, the phrase closing harmonically on an unexpected diminished
seventh. The effect is overwhelming:

Ex. 53

The voice ends inconclusively in the dominant from which the
instrumental *postlude* (violins only) takes over and dies away in a
hushed ecstasy:

Ex. 54

The concluding *adagissimo*, only twenty-five bars long, is so
extremely uncharacteristic and yet profoundly original that I quote
it in full:

Ex. 55

This is essentially pre-18th century music, and can only be explained by Handel's studies of his Italian predecessors and his obvious aim (perhaps by request) to give the music an ecclesiastical, even Romish, colouring. Never again was he to create music so withdrawn, so disembodied and introspective.

While we cannot cite *Ah! che troppo ineguali* as being typical Handel, it is nevertheless nearer the Handelian norm than the work just discussed. Chrysander for some reason excludes *Ah! che troppo ineguali* from the church music and places it among the cantatas (no. 26), though in an Appendix and with a query 'Frammento?' beside it. He then notes in his Preface that the work 'is probably not a fragment, but a sacred song composed to stand by itself'. While evidence is lacking, the work textually and stylistically claims kinship with the sacred antiphons. Although the shortest of them (consisting only of an introductory *recitative* and an *aria*), it is one of the supreme works of the composer's Italian period. Again we have the soaring intervals for the voice at the very beginning of the aria:

Ex. 56

The whole is permeated with an almost frenetic intensity, (helped
by the choice of key – b minor) with tritones and unexpected melodic
intervals and harmonic ambiguities abounding. Its chromaticism is
striking, and there is scarcely a bar without its suprising harmonic
and melodic twists. Two examples will illustrate this:

Ex. 57

Ex. 58

ed e stin - ta o - gni —— fa - cel - - la, fia del bel - -
- li - co fu - ror, fia del bel - li - co fu - ror___ al mor-

All these antiphons were written for soprano solo; and it becomes
evident from this and from the fact that of the finest arias in the
London operas by far the greatest number were also written for
soprano, that this was his favourite voice – as the contralto was
Bach's. Handel's sensitive ear told him that soprano was not only
the most flexible voice, but the most capable of conveying that
quality of 'soaring' and ethereality which was so integral a character
of his *cantilena*, particularly in his cantatas and operas. His predilection may or may not have been strengthened by the fact that the
most famous soprano of her time, Margherita Durastante, was
engaged by Ruspoli as principal singer. Rumour has come down to
us that Handel's association with her extended to the *extra muros!*
But even if it did, nothing came of it.

There remain of this group only two choral works to discuss. The
manuscript of the *Laudate pueri Dominum* is dated 8 July, 1707. This
D major setting for soprano solo, chorus and orchestra is a revised
version of a solo cantata in F major for high voice, two violins and
continuo which according to Chrysander is the earliest Handel
autograph extant (1703). The transformation of the ambling appren-
tice work of his Halle days into this later version makes a fascinating
study, and is a revelation of how far the young composer had come
in so short a time. While Doctor Fritz Stein in his Foreword to the
Peters edition of the work rightly points out that it evinces 'the
highly colourful and sensuous character of Roman Catholic church
music written in Italy in the late Baroque', and reveals the influence
of contemporary Italian composers, these aspects need not be

stressed, for the work is unmistakeable Handel, and there is not a
movement in it (with the possible exception of the 'Excelsus') which
could be taken for any other composer. Handel's own high opinion
of it may be deduced from the fact that he used the opening chorus
again in 1713 for his *Utrecht Jubilate* and the closing one in 1747 for
a chorus in *Joshua* ('Glory to God').

The work opens with a brilliant orchestral *ritornello* with strings
and oboes:

Ex. 59

At the sixteenth bar the solo voice enters. Some idea of the bravura
of the vocal writing can be glimpsed from the following typical
passage:

Ex. 60

After thirty bars the chorus enters, taking over the first theme and
the main interest, leaving the soloist with interspersed *coloratura*
interjections. The second number is a b minor solo: 'Sit nomen
Domini benedictum' with oboe *obbligato*, a quietly eloquent setting.
Bars forty-six to fifty-two illustrate a rare device in Handel – pro-
gression by diminished sevenths – here used with great effect in
dialogue between voice and instrument:

Ex. 61

The *forte* chord of G major which follows (*attacca*) the quiet b minor cadence and preludes the five part chorus: 'A solis ortu', and the announcement of the fugue subject by unaccompanied solo voice followed immediately by full choir and orchestra, show Handel's inborn dramatic sense and feeling for tonal colour:

Ex. 62

The following 'Excelsus super omnes' is the only movement in which the music falls below the highest Handelian standard. Written in the form of a gigue it might have stepped out of one of Corelli's violin sonatas, and is just a little facile. But with the brief five-part chorus: 'Quis sicut Dominus', we are reminded of the Handel of the *Dixit Dominus* written a year earlier:

Ex. 63

The verbal contrast of 'in coelo et in terra' brings a typical touch of *melisma*. Such possibilities were never missed by Handel:

Ex. 64

The A major solo which ensues: 'Suscitans a terra', scored for organ solo, two cellos and bass, is very Bachian in its long phrases and dark-coloured accompaniment, while retaining its essentially Handelian flavour. This leads without a break (*attacca* again) to another solo, but this time a bravura one, in the same key. Handel perhaps unconsciously recalled the opening solo phrase when writing the better known 'Oh! had I Jubal's lyre' forty years later.

Ex. 65

The final movement: 'Gloria Patri' for solo and chorus is both brilliant and subtle. After progressing for eighty-nine bars in 3/8 the movement makes an unexpected return to the 4/4 opening

'*Laudate*' sung by the solo voice but now to the words 'Sicut erat in principio', giving the work a unifying strength which adds enormously to its stature. Comparable with the Bach cantatas, this work, ebullient with youthful vitality and power, should be in the libraries of all self-respecting choral societies.

So we come to the last of these church works I wish to discuss – *Dixit Dominus*. The actual composition dates of many of these Italian works are uncertain, but we do know that the motet was first performed in Rome in the April of 1707. It was, therefore, in all probability the first of his major works to be written. But I have reserved discussion of it to the end of this section because it stands apart from the rest for two reasons: (1) its dazzling polyphony makes it the least Italianate in its style, revealing clearly Handel's German origins; (2) it is not only the greatest work of these years but one of the greatest of any year, not only of Handel but of any composer. Indeed, the more one studies the work the more overwhelming its craftsmanship and profundity become – and the fact that it is the production of a young man of twenty-two. That such a masterpiece can disappear for two hundred and fifty years and remain virtually unknown still, is one of those scandalous injustices which posterity seems to have reserved for Handel.

The work is scored for five-part chorus and string orchestra, with violoncello and organ continuo. The opening *ritornello* with its forceful character at once indicates Handel's sense of the importance of the orchestra and his unrivalled understanding of the tension and emotional power engendered by strings. Notice the brusque and surprising D♭. The refined smoothness of A. Scarlatti and Corelli is far away:

Ex. 66

The chorus begins with typical Handelian homophony. Then at bar fifty-two, following a full close of the orchestra in the relative major (B♭), the sopranos in unison, accompanied by violins I and II in unison, begin a *canto fermo*, while the other voices accompany with interjections on 'donec ponam inimicos':

Ex. 67

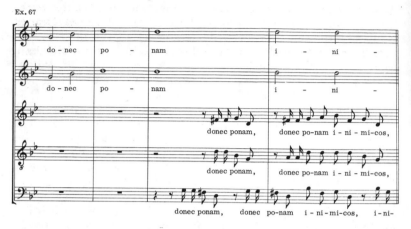

This melody, which has a liturgical flavour reminiscent of the old *a capella* school, is used again in the final chorus, 'Gloria Patri', giving the work a sense of all-pervading unity.

The alto and soprano solos which follow provide contrast to the massed vocal homophony. The soprano number in particular (again emphasising Handel's predilection for that voice) is deeply expressive.

The fourth number, 'Juravit Dominus', opens with five bars of harmony which must have caused Handel's contemporaries to regard him as the Schönberg of his day:

Ex. 68

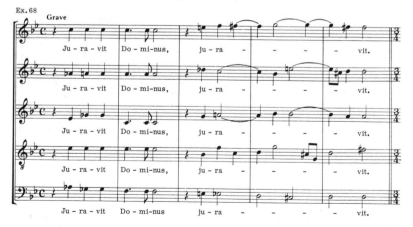

This 4/4 *grave*, breaking off on the chord of the dominant, plunges
into a 3/4 g minor *allegro* which in turn after sixteen bars dies away
to be taken over by the 4/4 *grave* reharmonised. But the 3/4 *allegro*,
now in d minor, has the last word. The concluding *ritornello* is worth
remarking for its unusual dynamics: *p*, *pp*, *ppp*. From this *pianissimo*
the Bb double fugue ('Tu es sacerdos in aeternum'), with its rising
bass, leaps into dynamic life:

Ex. 69

The sixth number, a d minor *allegro*, opens and continues with
heavenly suspensions between the first and second (solo) sopranos:

Ex. 70

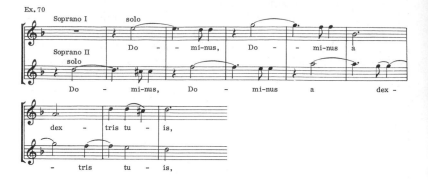

Supported over its full length of a hundred and thirty-two bars by a 'motor' bass, this *allegro* comprises some of the most original pages to be found in baroque music. Breaking off on a full close, it is followed without any introduction by a close-knit fugue in the relative major in 4/4 time on the words 'Judicabit in nationibus':

Ex. 71

but this proceeds for only sixteen bars when it is interrupted by an orchestral *ritornello* which, taking over in a flowing, typically Handelian style for eight bars, becomes the basis for the accompaniment to the rest of the chorus. Half way through the eighth bar the chorus enters with the words 'implebit ruinas', and the score rises to new heights of contrapuntal ingenuity. The episode terminates with a superb example of Handel's genius for the picturesque and dramatic in the *melisma* on the word 'ruinas', where the phrase tumbles from top to bottom like falling stones:

Ex. 72

At the same time the episode prepares us rhythmically for the final 'Gloria'. (The subtlety of Handel's methods of imparting unity to the work is worthy of the closest study). From the closing A major chord a new chorus, 'Conquasabit capita in terra multorum', flowers in d minor and in 3/4 (again without any introduction) and Handel proceeds to use all his declamatory skill to pile up slabs of five part block harmony on the word 'conquasabit':

Ex. 73

The seventh number, 'De torrente in via bibet', a c minor *adagio* for two solo sopranos against unison tenors and basses, constitutes some of the most moving and original pages ever composed. The

audience which heard the first performance of this work during the
Easter of 1707 must surely have been strongly moved by the brooding
mysticism and dissonant suspensions of this number:

Ex. 74

With it we re-enter that ethereal world conjured up by the *Salve
Regina*. Study of that work and this movement tempts one to believe
that this is the only music composed later than the 16th century to
recapture that sense of other-worldliness which seems to have been
the natural birthright of the *a capella* masters – Byrd, Palestrina,
Tallis, Gibbons, Victoria and Lassus.

There is nothing more thrilling in music, for performer and listener
alike, than the final 'Gloria' – a free, tremendous double fugue. The
opening *ritornello*, played by organ and lower strings in unison,
becomes used as counter-subject to the magnificent fugal entry of the
first sopranos:

Ex. 75

Handel loosens the tension, only to increase it again, by variation. At bar twenty-four he breaks off a three-bar orchestral *tutti* on the chord of the dominant to restart the fugue in the tonic with sopranos I and II singing the second subject in unison, and tenors the countersubject and – the final stroke of genius – basses the *canto fermo* of the first chorus:

Ex. 76

But Handel is not yet at the end of his resources. Another surprise awaits us at bar fifty-five where, after a full close in the relative major, a new fugal subject (*allegro*) is announced by the sopranos in unison:

Ex. 77

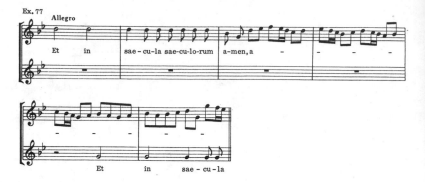

and this, taken up by the other voices, gains in complexity and momentum until at the 'Amen' the score becomes one of the most staggering examples of sheer craftsmanship ever written, and the movement closes in a triumphant blaze of sound and glory of counterpoint.

Dixit Dominus is not only the greatest work of Handel's Italian period: it is one of his greatest of any period and one of the pinnacles of choral music. Rarely, if ever, was Handel to equal, let alone surpass, the level of achievement reached by this work composed at the age of twenty-two. No one who has studied it will see any reason to doubt the legend that Mendelssohn, after borrowing the autograph score from the Royal Library, reverently kissed the manuscript before returning it.

The remaining small-scale works are comprised by the two Italian *Duetti* and *Terzetti*. But I propose to leave discussion of these to the last chapter for the reason that, of the twenty-two Italian Duos, only these two were actually written at this time, thirteen of the remaining twenty being composed at Hanover, and the rest in England between 1741 and 1745.[1]

There remain, then, the large-scale works to be considered, viz. the operas (*Agrippina* and *Rodrigo*), the oratorios (*La Resurrezione* and *Il Trionfo del Tempo*, and the serenata *Aci, Galatea e Polifemo*.

It was only to be expected that these should be the least successful from an aesthetic point of view. No young composer yet – not even the superlatively gifted and precocious Mozart, Schubert or Mendelssohn – has produced a satisfying first symphony, sonata, quartet, opera or oratorio. The vital mental discipline, expertise, architectonic sense, ability to maintain the essential unity along with

---

[1]See my *Chronological Thematic Catalogue*, nos. 29, 36, 129.

diversity, and diversity within the overall unity, to organise tonal unification and dramatic design, come only with experience gained from continual trial and error, from those initial failures so necessary for success. Even baroque opera, which to its more superficial and less knowledgeable critics may seem nothing but a string of recitatives and arias, needs these qualities, as comparison between these early examples of the genre and those of Handel's maturity (e.g. *Radamisto*, *Rodelinda*, *Ottone*, *Giulio Cesare*, *Admeto*) demonstrate. The same goes for the oratorios. Thus *Agrippina* (the success of which laid the foundation of Handel's European fame), *Rodrigo*, *Aci*, *Galatea e Polifemo*, *Il Trionfo del Tempo* and *La Resurrezione*, while all containing magnificent numbers,[1] are essentially heterogeneous, lacking any unifying scheme of tonality or dramatic pivot on which to develop. *La Resurrezione* in particular is a confused hodge-podge of styles. The orchestration is superb (employing in addition to the usual strings, flute, lute, oboes, trombone and clarini, and giving concertante numbers to viola de gamba and recorder); but there are only two choruses, both of them formal and perfunctory, and the arias vary not only in quality but in style. Lucifer's 'Caddi e ver' and Mary Magdalen's 'Per me già di morire' recall Bach in their Germanic seriousness, whereas the latter's 'Ferma l'ali' is so Italianate as to be able to form the generic theme of Mirtillo's 'Caro amor' in *Il Pastor Fido* without any sense of disparity. But the most notorious specimen of incongruity is the jaunty little air 'Hò un non sò che nel cor'. The fact that Handel was able to transplant this, words and all, into *Agrippina* and give it to the heroine to sing, is not a criticism in itself. For like Bach, he used the same arias for secular and religious purposes, and made no difference in terms of music between opera and oratorio. But a tune which could serve as a popular ballad[2] is, one feels, hardly one to give to Mary Magdalen as an expression of thanksgiving on the Resurrection! However that may be, Handel's patrons and audiences do not seem to have been upset by it, and the air became so popular that, like Figaro's 'Non più

---

[1]Especially *Rodrigo*, with five of Handel's most splendid arias: 'In mano al mio sposo', with its typical *cantilena*; the dramatic 'Stragi, morti;' the subtly canonic 'Fra le spine'; the brilliant 'Alle glorie'; and above all, Esilena's 'Empia fato', which he rarely surpassed for harmonic boldness and deftness of orchestration.

[2]'Signora Boschi also was evidently captivated by the air, made it her own property and took it to England, where, some months before Handel's arrival there, she introduced it into her part in Alessandro Scarlatti's opera *Pirro e Demetrio*. . . . Possibly the first thing Handel heard whistled in the streets of London was Mary Magdalen's little song . . . set to less seemly English words whose catchy little air had become a popular ballad'. (James S. Hall: *G. F. Handel* in The Great Masters series. Boosey and Hawkes).

andrai' some eighty years later, it was 'sung, whistled and hummed in the streets'.

Ex. 78

Hò un non sò che nel cor, che in ve-ce di do - lor, che in ve-ce di do-lor＿ gio-ja mi chie - dé. -dé. Hò un non sò che nel cor, hò un non sò che＿ nel cor, che in ve-ce di do - lor＿ gio-ja mi chie - di.

Despite their over-all immaturity, these first operas and oratorios of the young Handel show that he was a 'natural' with regard to dramatic works, with an inborn genius for achieving that triple essential without which no composer can hope to succeed in the genre, namely (1) fusion between voice and instruments, stage and pit, to which I have already referred (2) ability to transform subjective emotion into objective emotion in order to create stage characters able to express their own passions; and allied with these, (3) the discovery of an idiom which is a true expression of his own individuality as a composer and yet at the same time embraces the widest possible audience without sacrificing integrity. Not many composers have this natural 'voice', and still fewer all three attributes. But Handel is one of them.

HANOVER
(1710–12)

By the time the year 1710 came in Handel had another of his restless fits. He probably felt that he had learned all he could from Italy, and needed the stimulus of new circumstances and a new environment. Whatever the reason or reasons, we know that he accepted pressing invitations to visit England by the Duke of Manchester, Dusseldorf by the Elector Palatine and by both the Elector Georg Ludwig himself and his kapellmeister Steffani to take up residence at the court of Hanover. With typical opportunism, high sense of his worth and love of independence 'the Orpheus of our age' (as he was known in Italy) agreed to accept the Elector of Hanover's offer of 1500 crowns per annum on the condition that it did not prevent him from carrying out his promises to visit his other would-be patrons. Some idea of the universal esteem in which he was held can be gauged by the fact that the Elector granted him a year's leave of absence without a quibble. Soon after the agreement was clinched Steffani departed for Italy, leaving Handel as a very elusive court kapellmeister in his place.

Seeing that within the space of the first twelve months Handel took the opportunity to visit Halle to see his now blind and aged mother, Dusseldorf, to keep his promise to the Elector Palatine, and England (in the autumn) to oblige the Duke of Manchester, it is not surprising that the compositions attributable to the period of his actual stay at the Hanoverian court are few in number. The slight but charming *Sonata a 5* in B♭ for violin solo, oboes, strings and continuo, may well be one of them; it is possible that the three concerti for oboe, strings and continuo also date from this time. There can be no doubt, however, about the origins of the *13 Italian Duetti with Continuo*. We know that they were written expressly for Princess Caroline, who had a passion for indulging in vocal chamber works.

These Duos (and the two Duetti and two Terzetti dating from his years in Italy (see page 48 are important works, and as such deserve special consideration.

Just as A. Scarlatti had been Handel's model for the cantatas, so

Steffani was the main influence behind these vocal duos and trios. As with the cantatas, Handel was to surpass his model. Steffani's examples, although beautifully 'tailored' and singable, contain no such intensity of expression or harmonic boldness as is to be found in the very first bars of *Giù nei Tartarei regni*, where the clashing 'seconds' of the voices still comes as a shock to the listener even today, and to Handel's contemporaries must have seemed revolutionary:

Ex. 79

Nor does he produce such contrapuntal wizardry as is to be found in the *Terzetti*:

Ex. 80

The total achievement of these works represents a unique and unequalled contribution to this very limited genre. Compared with them most of the duets to be found scattered throughout the oratorios seem almost perfunctory. The over-all effect of these *duetti* and *terzetti*, despite passages of florid writing and expressive *cantilena*, is one of contrapuntal severity, and in their austerity of counterpoint and instrumental style at times strongly reminiscent of Bach. Like the latter's works, too, these are supreme examples of masterly craftsman-ship used solely for expressive purposes. They will repay endless study and are irrefutable proof – if such were ever needed – that Handel the craftsman is second to none. Technical mastery, perfection of form and, for a German-born composer, a quite miraculous ability to find a musical equivalent of the Italian text,[1] combine to make these works unique and unsurpassed. The general ignorance and neglect of them is inexcusable.

To sum up. The works of Handel's pre-England period (which may be said to end with his first London opera *Rinaldo* in 1710), have a two-fold importance. As I have tried to show, many of them are great in their own right, and the general ignorance and neglect of them is a blot on our musical culture which needs erasing, and the sooner the better. The value of them in the light of the music Handel was to compose in England throughout his life-time is incalculable. If as he grew older the religious influences of that period grew fainter and he tended more and more strongly towards a humanist phil-osophy[2] of which *Jephtha* is the ultimate expression, the Italian influences which went to make up his art never ceased from per-meating it. He was forever ransacking the drawers of his capacious memory to bring out something written then, in whole or in part, and adapting it to the need of the moment. Thus the highlight of his second oratorio, *Deborah*, the quartet with double chorus, 'All your boast', is based on the quartet 'Voglio Tempo' in *Il Trionfo del Tempo*; the lovely *Acis and Galatea* has its origins in the Italian *Aci, Galatea e Polifemo*; the orchestral accompaniment to the chorus 'But the waters overwhelmed their enemies' in *Israel in Egypt* is adapted directly from the aria 'Venti, fermate, sì' of the cantata *Armida abbandonata*; the 'Alleluia' of *Esther* and *Silete Venti* is a transplanta-tion from the antiphon *Saeviat Tellus;* Caesar's superb *coloratura* aria 'Qual torrente' owes its first seven bars note for note to 'A sanar le ferite d'un core' of the cantata *Fra tante pene*. Other examples too numerous to mention could be quoted, and it is perhaps symbolical that his ultimate opus, *The Triumph of Time and Truth*, dictated in his old age and blindness, should hark back to his early Italian *Il Trionfo del Tempo*. For Handel, the inspiration he received from Italy was a river which never ran dry, a vein which never ceased to yield ore. Even his most Germanic and English works never quite lost the Italian accent acquired in those three all-important years. It is as a result of that Italian influence that Handel is the composer above all others (Mozart alone, perhaps, excepted) in whom is to be found the perfect fusion of Italian *cantilena* and German polyphony to form a stylistic perfection that has never been surpassed.

---

[1]By Ortensio Mauro.
[1]Edward Fitzgerald's observation on Handel – 'he was a good old pagan at heart' – is worth remembering.

Only with the knowledge of these pre-England works, plus the London operas (which are of course a continuation and consummation of his Italian stage works) can the protean and colossal genius of this composer be seen steadily and seen whole. Those whose knowledge is limited to the English oratorios and anthems know only half the story.

INDEX

GENERAL INDEX